Beginners Guide To

Backyard Bird Photography

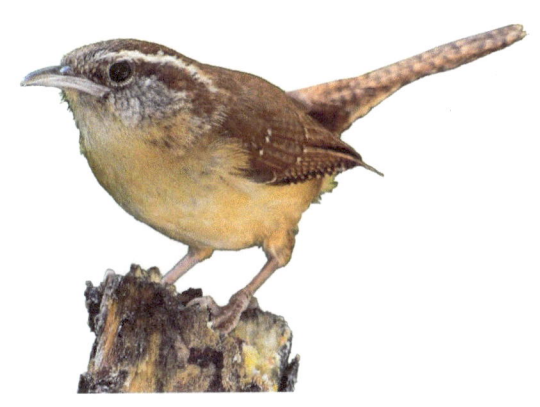

Mickey Estes

Hutchins House Publishing Co. LLC

Cover Design by Mickey Estes

Hutchins House Publishing Co. LLC

Dedication

To My Wonderful Wife

Suellen

What a privilege it has been to live these many years with such an outstanding woman, wife, mother, and Mimi [grandmother]. I bless my wife for all her love and understanding. We are truly one, and give the glory to our Lord and Savior Jesus Christ.

Thanks, Honey, for all the help you have given me.

Let's keep on Soaring together.

Mickey

Table of Contents

Introduction

According to a report by the U.S. Fish and Wildlife Service, there are 47 million bird watchers in the United States. And of these 47 million birders, 41 million of them are backyard birders. As an avid bird watcher myself, I began to combine this wonderful hobby with another one I have – photography - and ended up enjoying countless hours photographing backyard birds. In the process, I discovered that not only was it a lot of fun, but it also offered a therapeutic relief from stress and anxiety.

It's a lot like going fishing without having to clean the fish. Just as in fishing, you never know what you are going to catch.

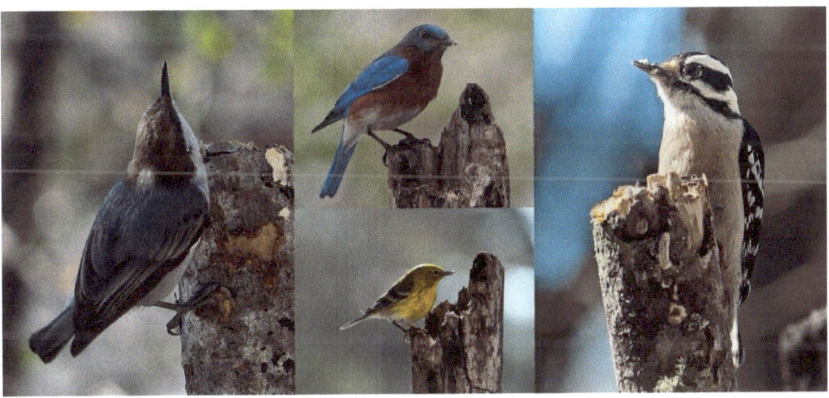

Over the years, the development of digital cameras has made backyard bird photography much easier. You get to review the results immediately, thus allowing instant critique of your last capture. This allows you to learn and improve as you go.

Often times when a new species visits the feeder, my first shots are just to capture it as documentation of its visit. As the bird returns to the feeder I become more artistic on how I capture its beauty. Eventually the first shots seem primitive when compared to the final photographs I get. These are those I call my "keepers."

It is because of this passion I have for bird watching and photography that I decided to write this quick guide. It is a combination of technical training and technique for ensuring beautiful photographs of the birds which visit your backyard feeders. Remember that bird photography is a work-in-progress. I think of it as rev 1, rev 2, etc. The more you do it, the more skill you acquire.

This guide is intended to pass on to you what I have learned in over 20 years of photographing birds. I am limiting this guide to backyard bird photography, with the primary scope being perching birds. As you grow in skill (and in camera equipment) you can move on to birds in flight or at nesting locations - such as photographing Eagles at their nest sites. Take your time in going through the guide. As you read something, then go and try it for yourself. Practice makes perfect. I hope that you will enjoy this great adventure as much as I do.

1

Knowing Bird Habits

Take the time to observe different bird species and learn their habits. Each type of bird has its unique habits, and the more you learn about these the more successful you will be in photo capture.

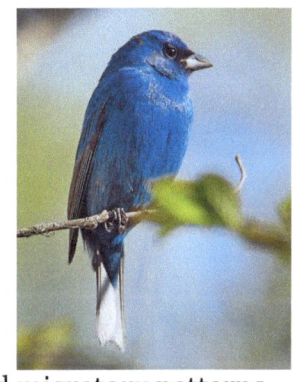

Some factors that affect bird habits are time of day, weather patterns, seasons, temperature, people population (rural or urban), frequency of visits to the feeder, and migratory patterns.

Spring is a great time for bird photography. During this season, the mating colors come to fullness and the male birds are paying more attention to their gals than to you. Thus they don't notice your activity as much. It is also the time for migration, so you may see species at the feeder which normally are not common to the area.

During winter, food is not as plentiful, so more species of birds are likely to come looking for food. Birds are more active in feeding in midmorning (8-10 AM) and late evening (4-6 PM) but will come to the feeder throughout the day.

11

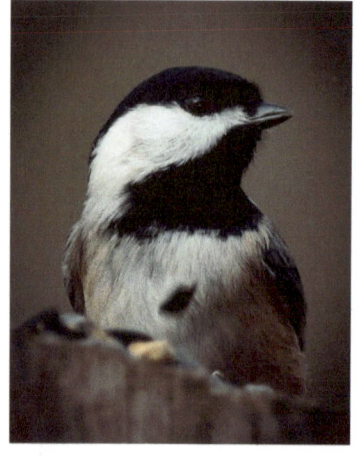

Some species seem to be tamer (Nuthatch, Chickadee, Cardinal, Finch) than others (Titmouse, Red-bellied Woodpecker).

Some birds are ground feeders, some perch on limbs, and some climb. Observing these habits helps you to determine the best ways to draw the birds closer and capture them in your photographs.

Birds watch each other and will find your food sources by seeing other birds flying in to your feeder.

The types of food you use will attract different types of birds. My primary food source is Sunflower seeds. I think this is a favorite of most seed-eating birds. My second most popular food source is Suet.

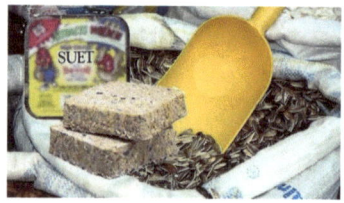

In the winter time, Suet will attract both seed and insect eating birds. Suet is a primary energy source for birds in winter because of the high fat content. For this reason, many birds which normally would not go to feeders (Mocking Bird, Catbird, Wren, etc.), are more likely to visit a Suet feeder.

Getting Closer

In bird photography you want the image of the bird in the photograph to be big enough for someone to see it. People have shown me photos of a bird which they have taken with their cell phone. "See the bird? Can you identify it?" ... Identify it?! I can't even see it!

To get large images you either need BIG lenses or you need to get the birds closer to you. Many people, when buying a digital camera, get a zoom lens with it - maybe 200mm (4X) or 300mm (6X) lens. This is good enough if you can get the bird within about 10 feet. (I will discuss some ways to do this later).

Shown below is a magnification chart which compares the distance of the bird to the camera, and the lens magnification necessary for equivalent size. As can be seen, closer is better - and cheaper. I can take a picture at 6 feet with a standard 55-200mm zoom lens (cost of about $200), that would require a 600mm lens (cost of $10,000 and higher) at 24 feet. As mentioned above, the trick is to draw them to you.

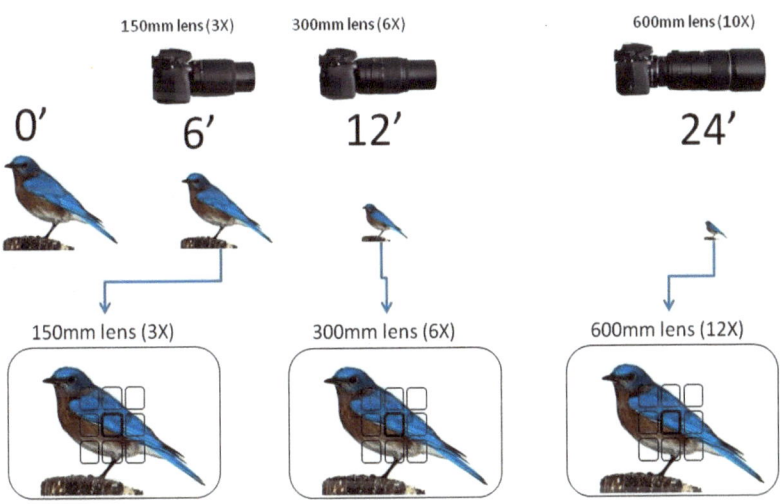

One of the most important concepts to
understand is Depth of Field

2

Terms and Explanations

Before we start on technique, I would like to go over some terms used in this guide to help give you a clear understanding of meanings. This is not meant to overwhelm you with technical jargon, but to give you some basic knowledge of the process.

TP (Target Point)

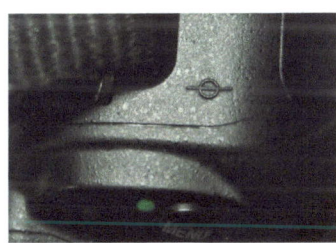 When a camera focuses, it focuses on a TP (Target Point) a certain distance from the surface of the film, or now, the digital sensor. A lot of cameras actually have a mark on the camera to designate where the focal plane on the camera is located so that you can line it up with the TP.

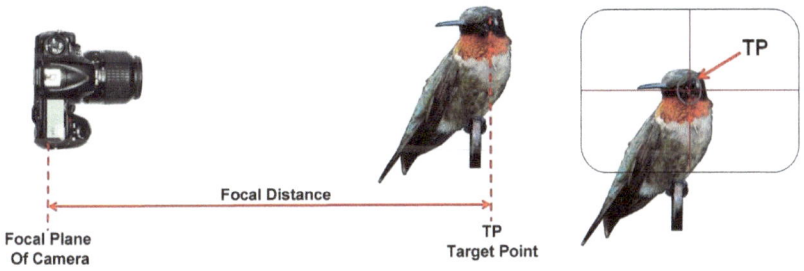

Focal Distance

Focal Plane
Of Camera

TP
Target Point

TP

This TP (Target Point) is the point on which you want to focus the camera.

DOF [Depth of Field]

Depth of Field is how much is in focus in front of and behind the Target Point. It is very important to understand DOF. It is a critical factor when doing bird photography and determines *"how much is in focus"*.

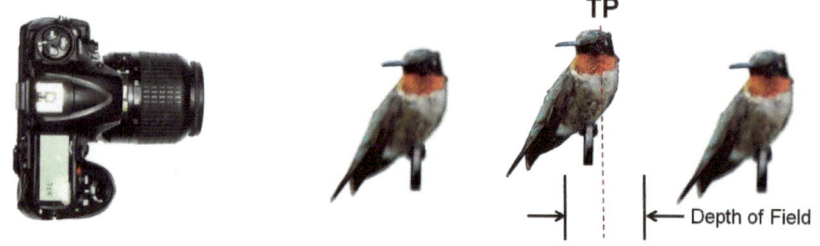

Depth of Field is determined by the focal length of the lens, the aperture setting, and the distance from the TP. Shown below is a comparison of DOF based on different focal lengths.

Depth of Field   Focal Length

Comparison of DOF for 6 focal lengths at same aperture and distance.

Aperture = 5.6 Distance = 10 feet

TP

Focal Length	DOF		
28mm	10.7	feet	
50mm	2.7	feet	
100 mm	.67	feet	8 inches
200 mm	.16	feet	1.9 inches
300 mm	.069	feet	.8 inches
400 mm	.037	feet	.4 inches

Here is another illustration of calculated DOF. Calculations were computed for 200mm and 300mm lens at 7 feet at various f-stops. Pay attention to the huge difference between DOF for the two lenses. This is why DOF and focus are so important.

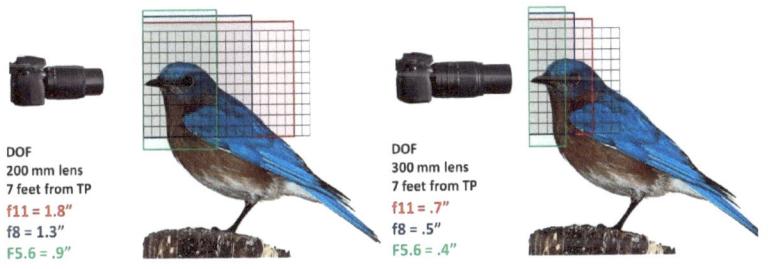

DOF
200 mm lens
7 feet from TP
f11 = 1.8"
f8 = 1.3"
F5.6 = .9"

DOF
300 mm lens
7 feet from TP
f11 = .7"
f8 = .5"
F5.6 = .4"

The illustration below shows how the position of the bird can affect what is in focus. Side shots are always better if possible.

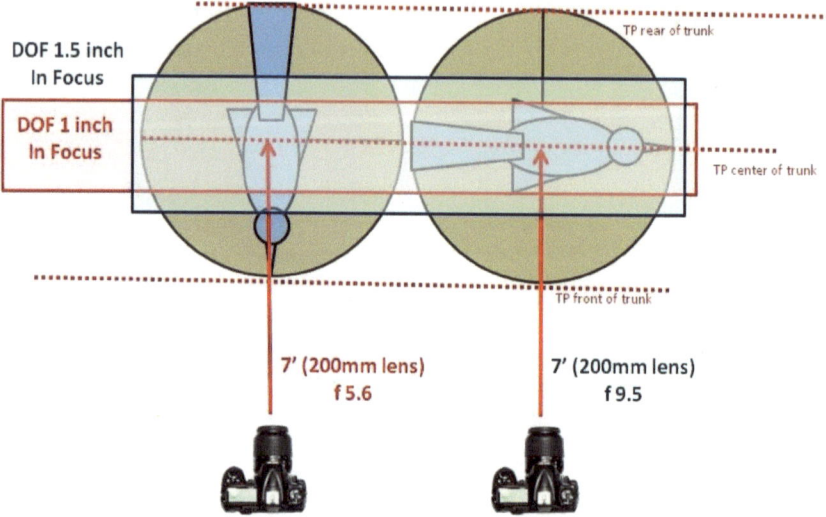

1. If you use manual focus – focus on center of trunk prop.
2. Try to take side shots of bird as much a possible. More of the bird will be in focus.
3. This also holds true using Autofocus. Side shots are better when possible.

Aperture (f-Stop)

Aperture, or f-stop, is a term used to describe the hole size on the lens which determines how much light you are letting into the sensor through the camera lens. Each lens has a set of blades on the inside that rotate open and closed.

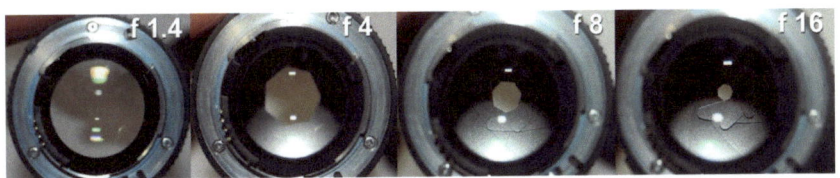

The photographs above show how these blades open and close to adjust the amount of light coming into the sensor. The smaller the f-stop number, the larger the hole size. For each change in f-stop,

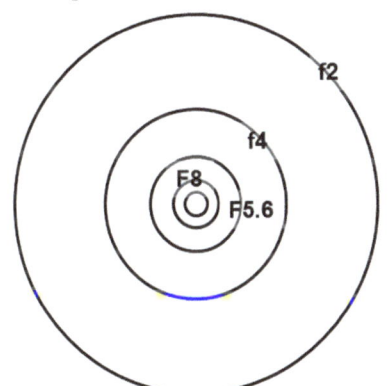

the hole either doubles or halves in size. This can be seen on this illustration. Notice how much the hole sizes change with each change in f-stop. The more expensive lenses have the lower f-stops, thus the larger holes letting in more light. We call these "Fast Lenses." They are very expensive compared to stock f 5.6 lenses, but are necessary for faster shutter speeds and use with teleconverters. Fast lenses seldom lose their value over time. As you progress in your photography skills, you may want to consider buying a Fast prime lens.

Camera Focus Patterns

Most of the newer digital cameras have a variety of focus modes. The three most common are spot, center weight, and full.

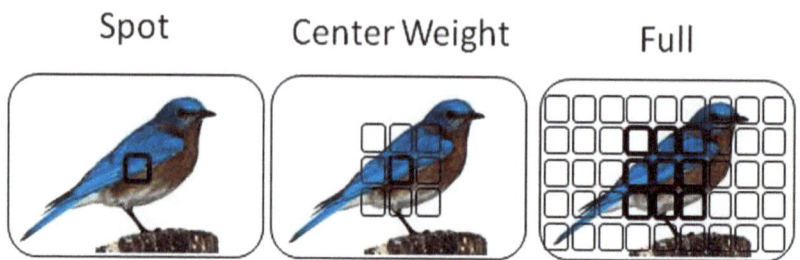

I almost always use spot or center weight when I focus on birds from behind the camera [not using a remote]. Normally I use spot and focus on the eye with the shutter release button pressed halfway down. Then I recompose the picture and take the photograph.

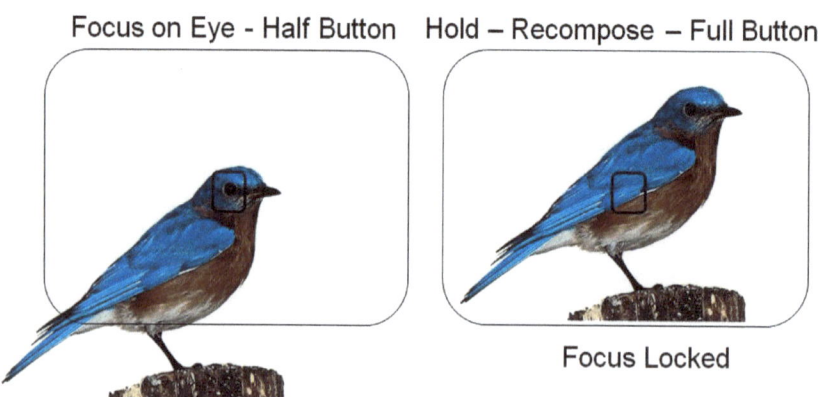

Camera Exposure Metering

Again most newer digital cameras have a lot of different settings you can use for proper exposure. As with the focus pattern, the common exposure patterns are similar: spot, center weight, and full metering.

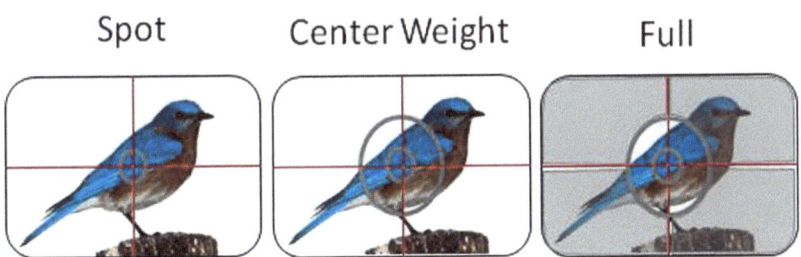

Because of the fact that proper exposure of the bird is the most important exposure factor, I use spot or center weight metering. Once you have selected the metering mode you want, the exposure is preset the same way the focus is set. Using spot metering, I aim at the bird's eye, press the shutter release halfway down, recompose the image location, and full press the shutter release to take the photograph.

ISO

In Digital Photography **ISO** measures the sensitivity of the image sensor. The same principles apply as they do in film photography - the lower the ISO number, the less sensitive your camera is to light and the finer is your image grain. The higher **ISO** settings are generally used when more shutter speed is desired at a given aperture, or when it is darker.

Exposure Triangle

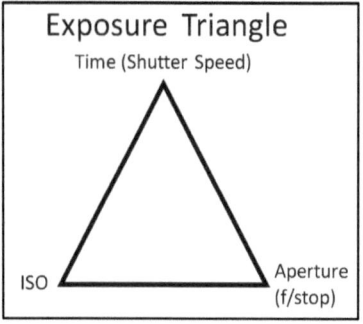

The exposure triangle shows the three components of Exposure. If you keep any one of the three (Time, Aperture, ISO) constant, the other two will change relative to each other.

In the illustration on the facing page, the relationship between ISO, Aperture and Time (shutter speed) are shown for a given EV (Exposure Value) or light condition. All of the three exposure settings in f-stop and Time will give you the same properly exposed photograph. For each change in f-stop, you either double or halve the time the shutter stays open. As can be seen in the illustration, as the aperture doubles in hole size, the time of exposure is halved. In this illustration the EV and ISO are constant.

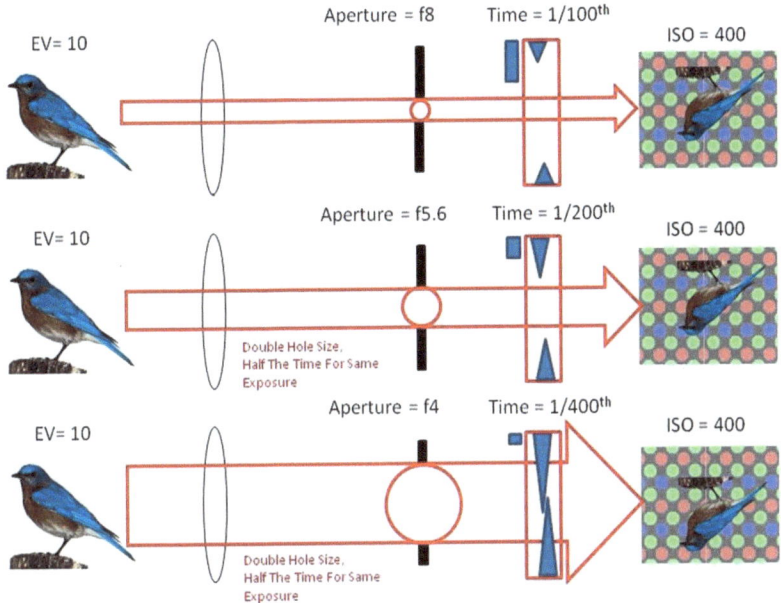

Below is another illustration that shows the relationship between aperture (hole size) and time (shutter speed).

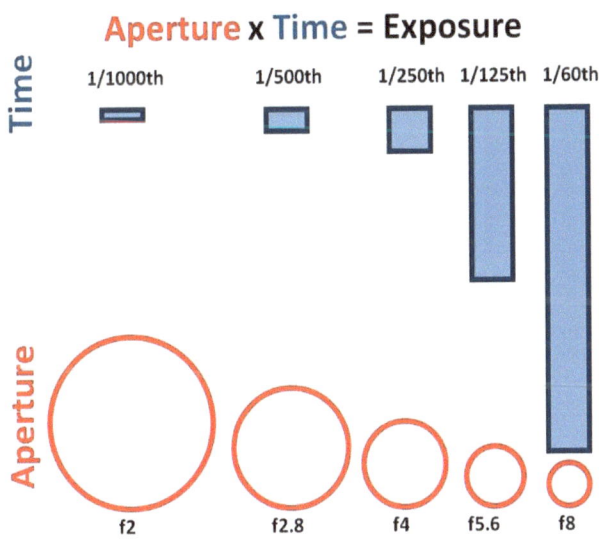

Crop Factor

Before digital cameras came along, the most popular film camera used film referred to as 35mm, which had a frame measurement of 36x24 mm. This became a standard so that when camera lenses were rated for their focal lengths (e.g 24mm, 55mm, 200mm) the ratings were based on the 35 mm film size. When digital cameras came out, the sensors in the cameras were not the same size as the older film (35m), so the same lens would produce a different size image on different size sensors. This is what we refer to as Crop Factor.

Most DSLR [Digital Single Lens Reflex] cameras now either have an FX (full size 35mm equivalent) sensor or DX (APS ~22x15) smaller size sensor. With the FX sensor, the image produced would be equivalent to the 35mm film camera, so the crop factor would be 1. When the same lens is used on the smaller camera sensor (APS), then the crop factor would be 1.5 to 1.6. The bottom line is that when you use a 200mm lens on a DX format camera, it will be equivalent to using a 300 mm lens on an FX camera.

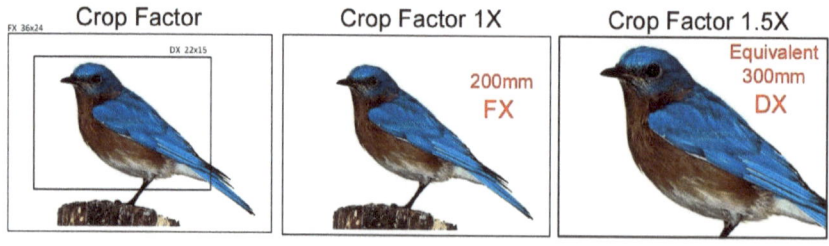

Image Compression (format)

When an image is captured by a camera, the image is saved in an image format. Typical formats will be JPEG, TIFF, and RAW. The more an image is compressed, the more of the metadata is lost. If you save images in RAW format, which basically is an uncompressed format, all the exposure information is saved. This means that when you post process the image you can change a lot of the exposure parameters and finely adjust the image. The JPEG format is the most compressed and the most limited as to which exposure settings you can change. RAW files take up a lot more room than the JPEG files.

Some cameras allow you to save in two formats. Most of the time I save in JPEG and RAW. I also save the picture in the highest resolution (largest image size). After post processing, I can delete any photographs I do not care to keep.

Using Props to draw and position birds greatly enhances your chances of getting Exceptional Bird Photographs

3

Methodology of Photographing Birds

There are three different ways I do backyard bird photography.

1) **On Site** - Go to where the birds are and set up [tripod used].

2) **Post/Branch/Feeders** - Bring the birds to me [tripod, monopod, or handheld].

3) **Freelance walk around** [usually handheld - bigger lenses].

On Site

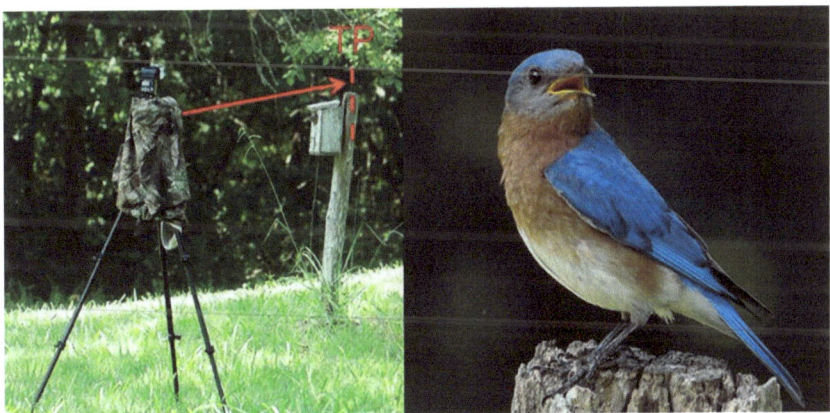

In the first method example, I used a bluebird nesting box and set up with a telephoto lens and a remote shutter release. I used both manual settings and auto settings during the photo session. I draped a camouflaged shirt over the camera body to ease the bird. In the cases where the TP was on top of the post, I used manual focus on a predetermined spot. This kept the camera from focus hunting, as it might do in autofocus.

Once again, to photograph the Goldfinch, I set up on a predetermined TP after observing the bird's habits. There was a favorite spot where the birds liked to land and perch before going to the seed.

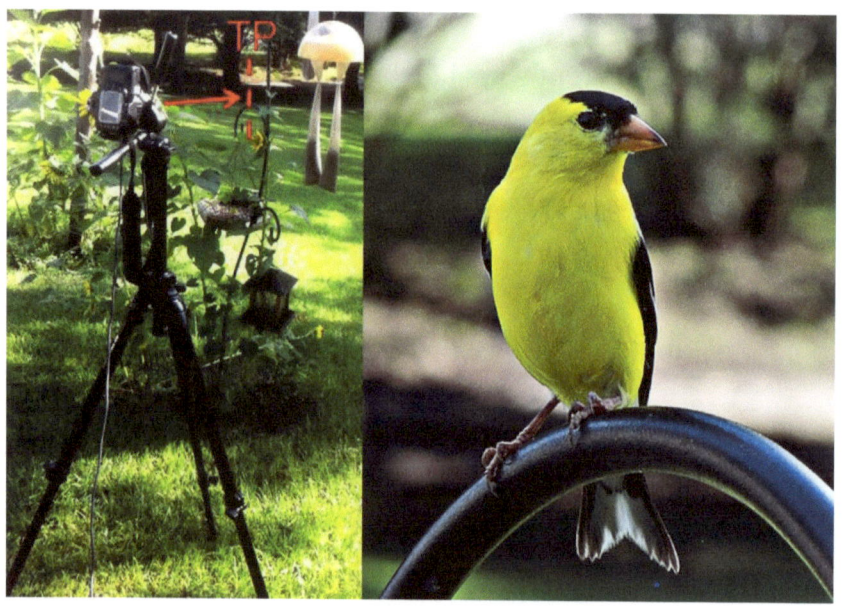

Once I set up the camera using a cable shutter release, I just sat in the shade and waited for the Goldfinch to arrive on the feeder.

The photograph below was taken by setting up the camera on a Cardinal's nest through my kitchen window. The cardinal had built a nest in a bush close to the window. I set up the camera with a telephoto lens on the kitchen table looking through the window, turned off the kitchen light, and waited for feed time. Using a remote shutter cable allowed me to take the photograph without bothering the father Cardinal. I Used flash, autofocus, and autometer.

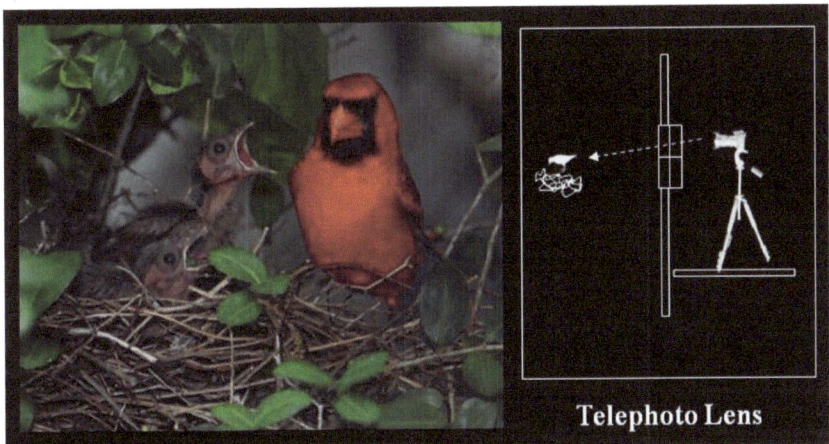

Telephoto Lens

Post/Branch/Feeder

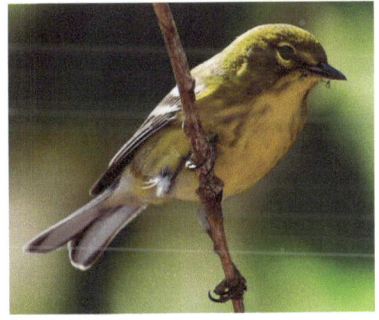

Given the chance, most birds like to fly to a perch and then to the feeder. Unless you have a flat feeder, birds feel more comfortable landing on a surface (post or limb) before going to the feeder. So I place a Prop (post or limb) close to the feeder and use that as my TP (Target Point) to set all my exposure and focus parameters. In some cases, the posts themselves are used as feeders.

I will talk about this in more detail later.

Below are several setups I have used with lots of success

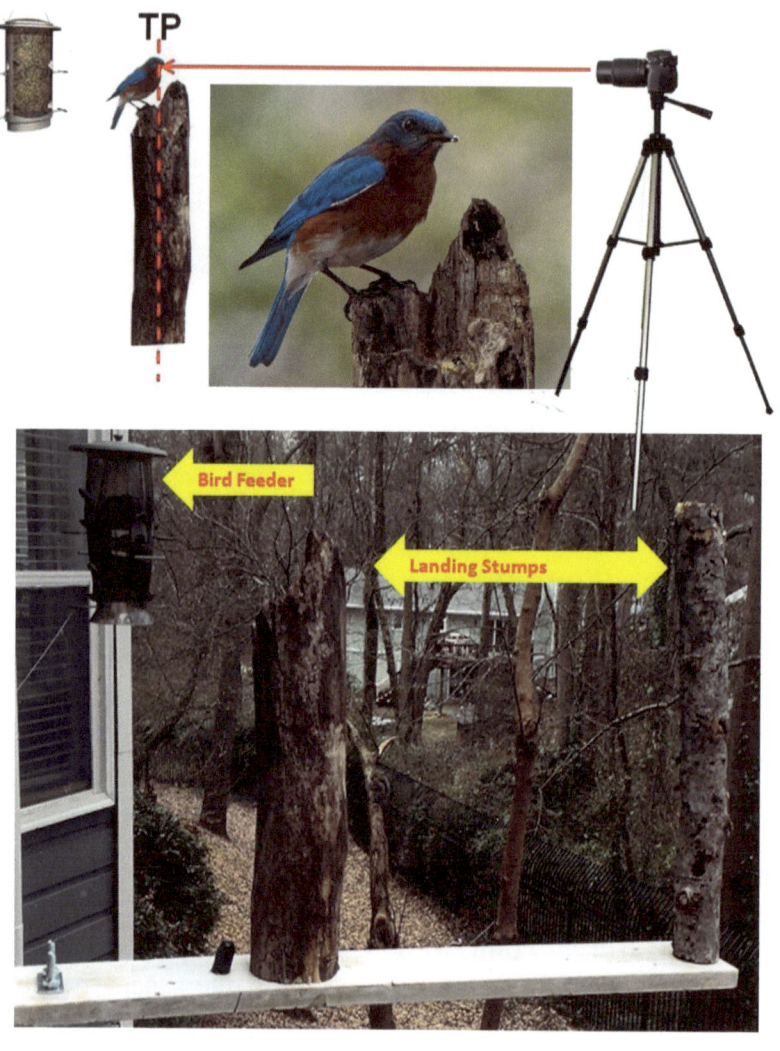

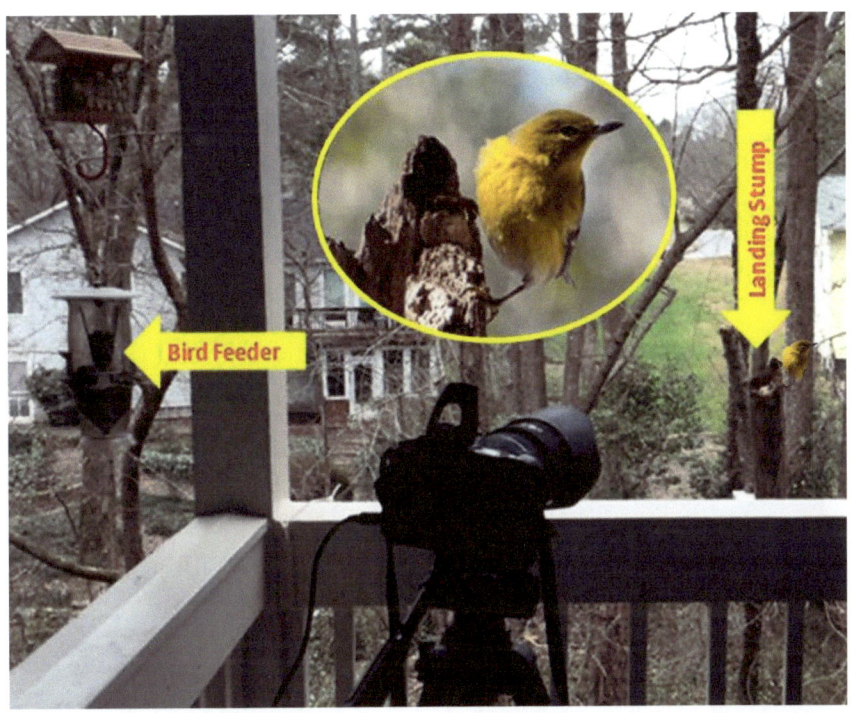

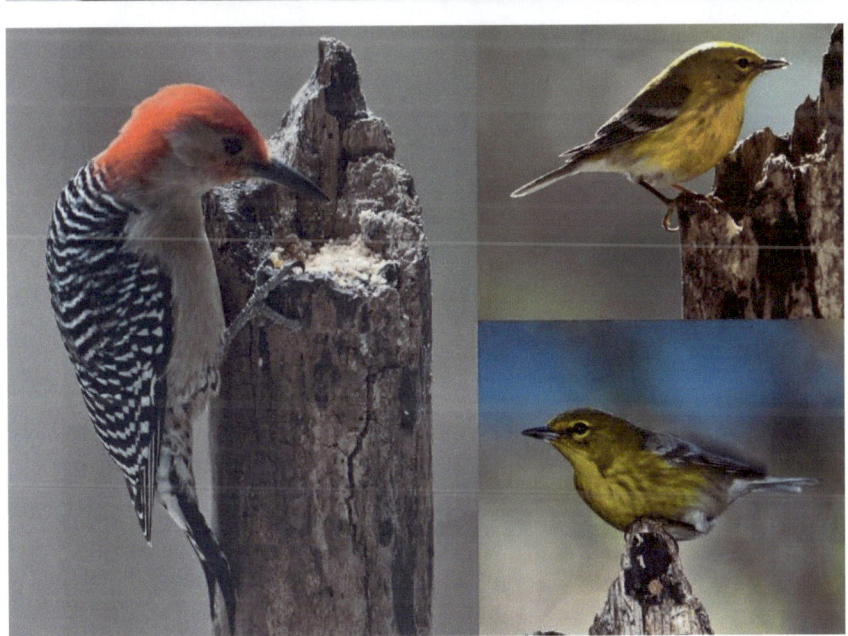

In this setup I used old tree parts mounted to a board and attached to my back deck. I then put Sunflower seeds and suet in the cavities, which drew the birds to feed. I was limited as to the direction of the prop in regards to the sun position. This was not a problem as long as I used some fill flash to correct for shadows.

Humming Birds

When photographing Humming Birds, I noticed that a dominant bird liked to sit close to the feeder to ward off other birds. If you can set up a dummy limb sticking out of the ground close to the feeder, many times the bird will perch there to protect the feeder. You can almost train them to come to a spot based on where you locate the feeder. Taking time to do this can yield some great photographs.

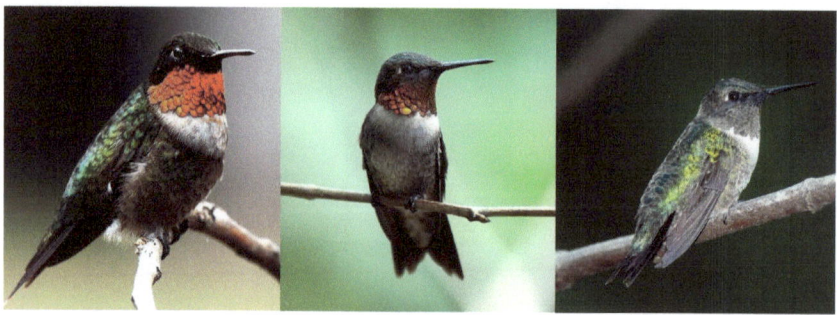

Freelance

Just walking around with a camera in your hand can yield some pretty nice photographs. However, you will need some good magnification (300mm lens or above) to get any decent image size. Teleconverters can help as long as they don't significantly reduce the quality. The stock f5.6 zoom lenses will do fine in bright light, but in shade and early morning/late evening they may be more challenging. With the newer cameras you can go up in the ISO setting (~1600) and that will give you some shutter speed advantage in the lower light.

I would recommend using a monopod when possible, to help stabilize the camera. This also helps with the weight of the camera-lens combo, when you are waiting a long time to get that perfect shot.

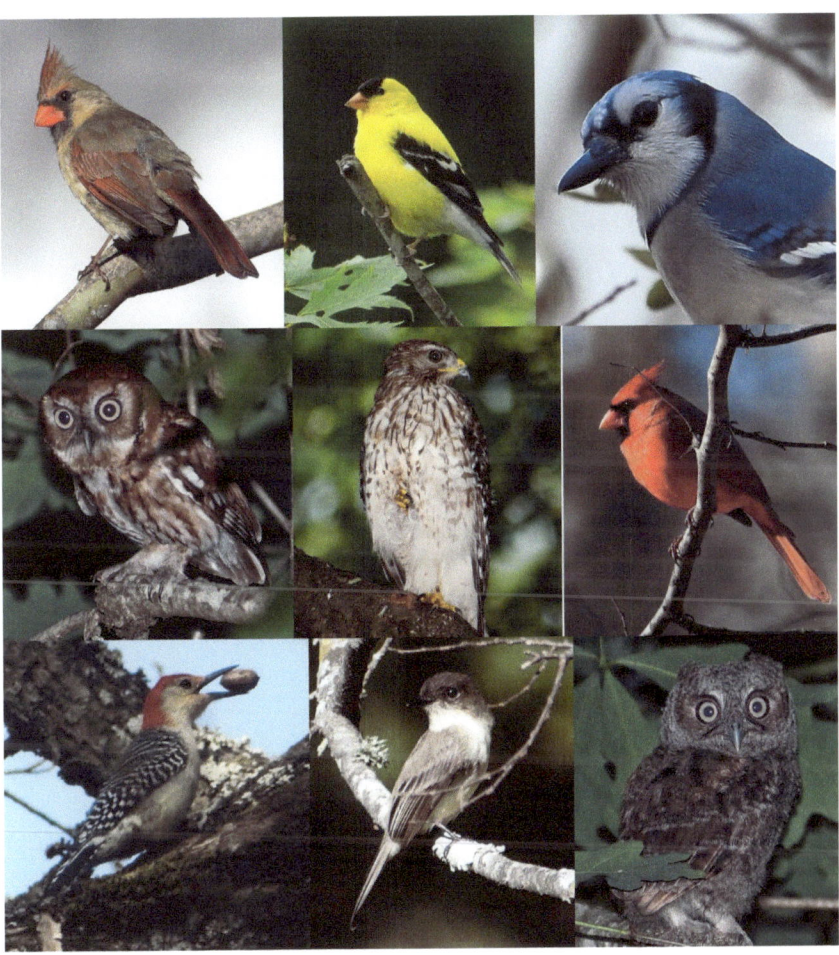

When there is plenty of light outside, Teleconverters can be very useful with telephoto lenses

4

Creating a Backyard Studio

I like to control the area where I want to photograph birds, and you can too. Start by looking at the lay of the land. Ask yourself where you want to set up your camera and where you want the birds to come. Bird feeders are the tools you use to bring the birds to you.

It's like setting up a Backyard Studio.

Factors to consider:

- Where do you want to set the camera (inside through open window, outside)?
- How far away or close to the TP do you want to be? (6' – 10' max).
- How isolated is the TP? If you plan to use a remote shutter release, you must have a very small area (TP) where the bird lands, so it will be in view when you take the photograph.
- How does the sunlight fall on the TP? Avoid direct sunlight, if possible. It gives too much contrast. Be sure to consider morning sun and evening sun. If I have a choice, I always choose morning sun.
- Which direction is the sun when you plan to do most of your photography? Best to have the sun behind you, shining on the TP that faces you.

- What does the background look like? This is so important. You want the background to be as non-descript as possible. Is it light or dark?

Once you have decided the approximate position you want the TP to be, you can start constructing your Backyard Studio.

How to Make a Prop

Post

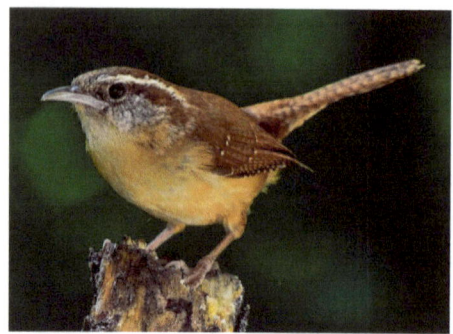

There are many ways to make props on which birds can land in order to take photographs at a designated TP. The ones which are going to be feeding posts or limbs can be designed so that the food is not very obvious. If you want to use a post close to the feeder, try to find an old farm post or something that looks rustic. Then drill a hole in the top (hidden as much as possible) for Sunflower seed or suet. When the birds land to feed, the food is recessed, and not visible to the camera.

Tree Trunk or Limb Props

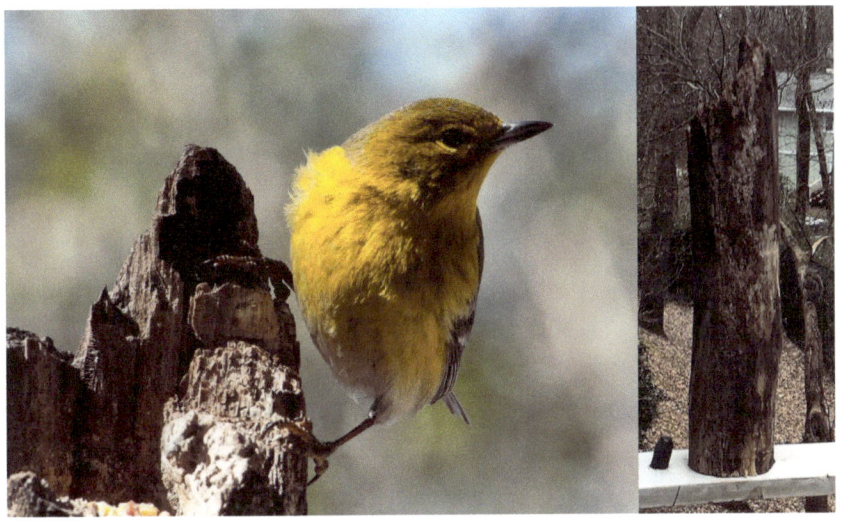

I started using cut pieces of trees several years ago because I wanted to mount something off my deck that I could use as a prop for bird photography. Again, if you can find an old broken end of a branch and the end is weathered, you'll have a terrific prop. The picture of a Pine Warbler (above) is a good example of how this looks. (Earlier in the book I showed pictures of this set up).

There are a few things I learned as I was making these tree trunk props. If you leave a small limb on the main trunk and drill a hole about 3" above the limb, it invites birds that perch (Catbird, Cardinal, Blue Jay, Mocking Bird, etc.) to feed on the trunk. The more types of birds you attract, the more exciting your photography venture will be. Below is a drawing to illustrate this. Drill holes and place the rotation of the trunk so that the food source is hidden.

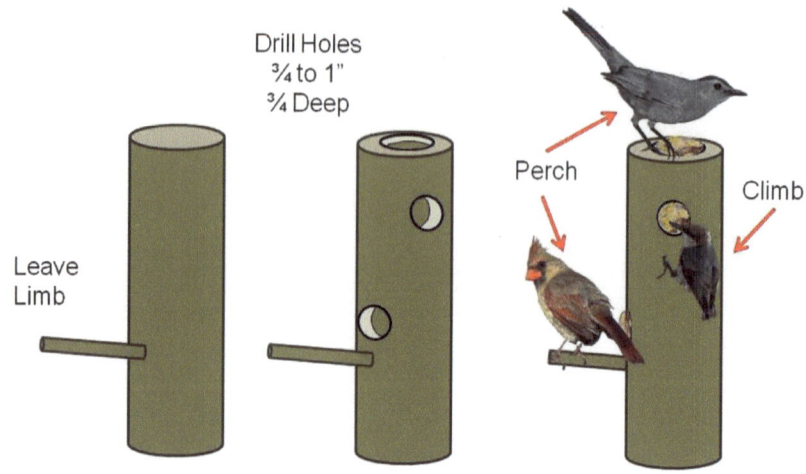

Leave Limb

Drill Holes ¾ to 1" ¾ Deep

Perch

Climb

When you plan to do a lot of remote shooting, it is better to have only one feeding hole on the trunk prop. This will limit where the bird will land and feed. Also, rotate the trunk so that the hole is out of sight of the camera. For top holes, angle the camera below the top of the trunk to help conceal the feeding hole.

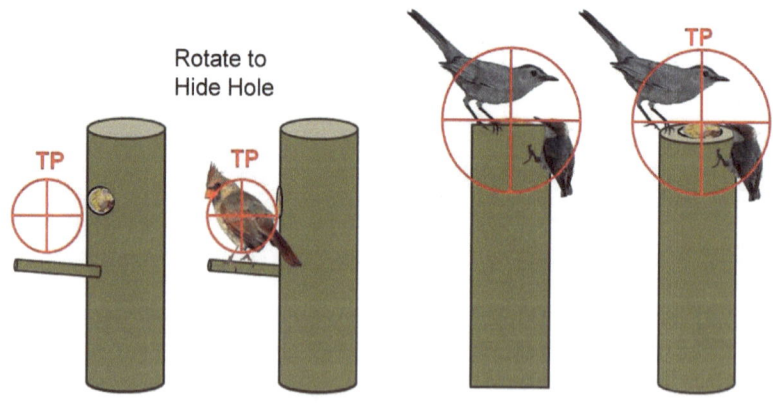

Rotate to Hide Hole

Assembly and Mounting of Trunk Prop to Deck Rail

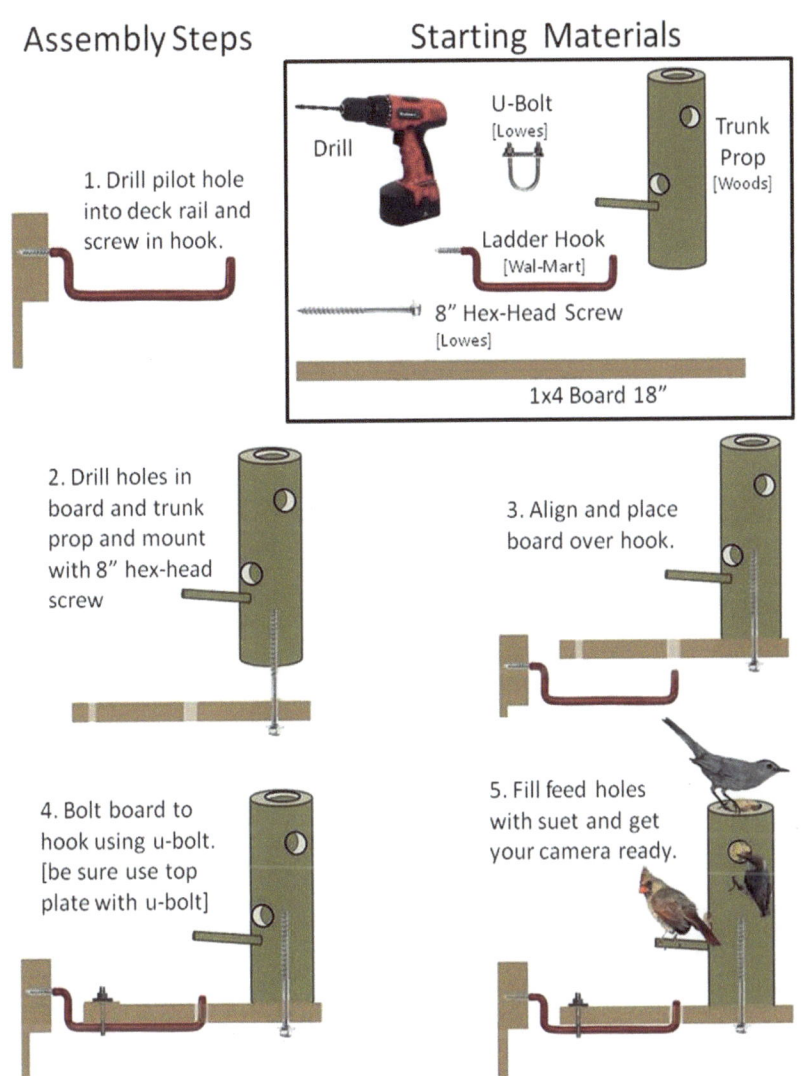

Assembly Steps

Starting Materials

1. Drill pilot hole into deck rail and screw in hook.

Drill

U-Bolt
[Lowes]

Trunk Prop
[Woods]

Ladder Hook
[Wal-Mart]

8" Hex-Head Screw
[Lowes]

1x4 Board 18"

2. Drill holes in board and trunk prop and mount with 8" hex-head screw

3. Align and place board over hook.

4. Bolt board to hook using u-bolt. [be sure use top plate with u-bolt]

5. Fill feed holes with suet and get your camera ready.

Simple Branch Prop

The simplest prop can be a small branch mounted on a deck rail close to the feeder. The birds will begin to fly to this branch before going to the feeder. I took this picture just sitting on the back porch hand-holding my camera. I had the flash up and manually set to 1/8 power. I took a few test shots on the branch itself just to check the exposure, and then just waited for my little friends to show up while enjoying a beautiful fall afternoon.

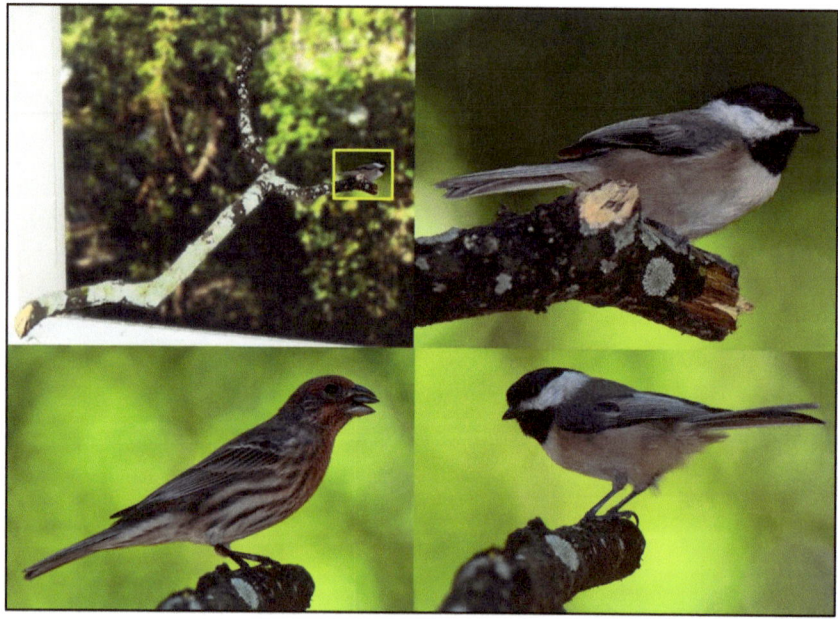

5

Photographing Technique

Remote Shooting vs Behind the Camera Shooting.

When possible I always like to be behind the camera so I can view and frame the bird before I take the photographs. This is often possible if you have a telephoto lens that allows you to be far enough away (6-10') so as not to spook the bird. I have done this many times using a stock f5.6 VR lens, hand-held. You will find over time that some types of birds will become tame and come to the TP with you close by.

I like to have the camera mounted on a monopod and sometimes I use a wired remote shutter release. This allows me to sit, hold, and focus with maximum comfort (after a while that camera and lens can get heavy), and to do it with less motion. One rule of thumb I use is always to move very slowly around the bird and avoid any gestures or sudden movements which will scare the bird. These types of actions have a reverse effect on the bird becoming tolerant of your presence.

Manual Exposure

Most of the time I set up my exposure in manual setting. This sounds scary, but with digital photography you can view the photograph instantly and make adjustments until you have the correct exposure. Review the histogram of the photo if you really want to fine tune the exposure. In most cases there will not be gross shifts in light intensity EV (Exposure Value) during the time frame you have allotted for taking photographs. The exception is when a lot of clouds are passing by, casting shadows on the TP.

When I set up to do a shoot, I do test shots in manual setting - adjusting shutter speed, aperture, and ISO (sensor sensitivity). These are the three factors at a given EV (light intensity) which determine proper exposure. On occasion, if you feel the light is changing, just run some more test shots.

If this still makes you nervous and you want to use the exposure metering system on the camera, then set the exposure meter setting on SPOT focus. In this setting the camera meters a very small target area and sets exposure based on that measured area. By spot metering on the bird, you have a high probability of having correct exposure for the bird.

Using a Flash

Most of the time I use fill FLASH in photographing birds. The flash exposure value is set manually and adjusted based on how the test shots look. I usually set the flash exposure between 1/4 and 1/32 power, depending on how far the camera is from the TP and how bright it is outside. The idea is for the flash to illuminate some of the shadow with fill light. This reduces the contrast in the photograph and enhances the color of the bird. It also helps pick up detail in the eye of the bird.

I never use the TTL (through the lens metering) flash setting when taking bird photographs. When TTL is used, the camera fires off the flash and measures the flash exposure through the lens, adjusts the power setting of the flash, and then fires off a second time with the correct metered flash exposure. The problem that I have found using this method of flash exposure is that the bird is spooked with the initial test flash, so that when the second flash is fired and the photograph taken, the bird is fluttering or flying away. This leaves you with a very disappointing photograph of a blurry flapping bird. Trust me: set up your flash manually.

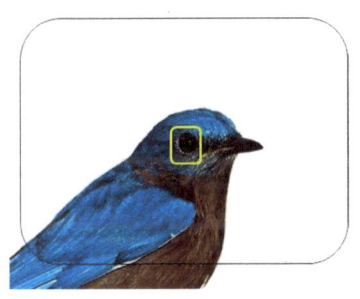

Focus

Most bird photographers will tell you that the EYE is the most critical part of the bird to be in focus. When I use autofocus I set the focus mode to SPOT or Small Area. If I am sitting behind the camera I will aim the SPOT focus area at the bird's eye, then hold the shutter release button half way down in order to lock the focus. I then reposition the view to include the whole view I want and press the shutter release button all the way down to take the photograph. This method ensures that the eye of the bird will be in sharp focus.

When you are shooting with a remote, the above is not possible. As a matter of fact, when you are shooting with a remote, you usually cannot use the Autofocus of the camera because you are not sure which part of the bird will be the point of focus. In these cases of using a remote it might be better to use a larger focus area

43

than that of SPOT. You must keep in mind exactly what the camera is seeing in the focus area.

For example, if you have positioned the camera above a limb or post top expecting that when the bird lands it will be in the camera view, care must be taken. You must be certain that when you press down on the prefocus button, the camera actually sees the bird and is not looking beyond to the background. If this happens the camera will refocus on the background and not the bird. The resulting photograph will have the bird out of focus.

Manual Focus

When I use manual focus, I anticipate where the bird will be and then prefocus to that point. As I do this I have to be mindful of the DOF (Depth-of-Field) - the amount of distance that will be in focus in front of and behind the TP (Target Point). This is discussed in greater detail in the technical section. If you are using a telephoto lens and are at a close distance, the DOF will be very small, so the manual focal point is critical. *[Review the DOF chart in the Terms & Explanations Section]*

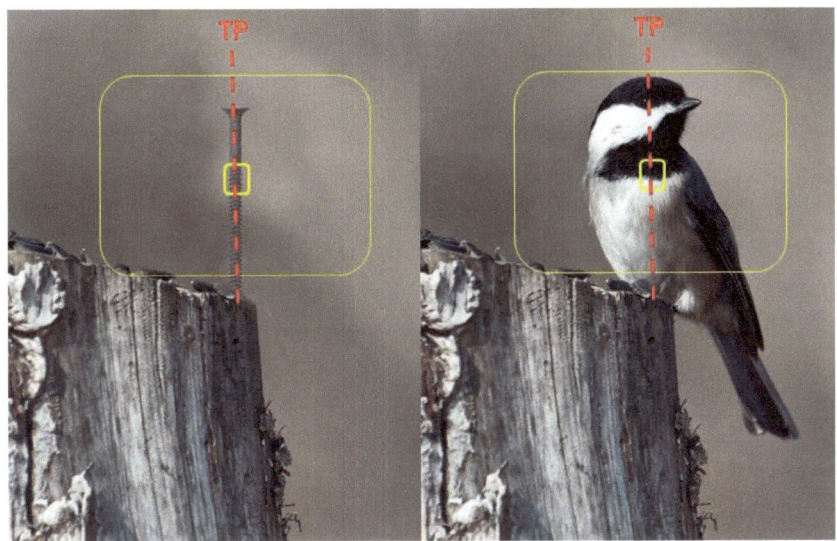

An example would be as follows: I am taking a photograph of a Chickadee landing on the top of a post sprinkled with Sunflower seeds in order to draw the bird. I will assume the bird will land on the edge of the post to pick up the seed. I would then manually focus the camera to the edge of the post. To do this accurately, I may drive in a screw a few turns, focus on the screw head manually, then remove the screw, put down the seeds, and wait on my subject. (For an easier method, you may place a small object at the TP and focus on the object). Having prefocused, and set exposure and flash, I am ready to capture a great photograph of a Chickadee as he darts in to get the Sunflower seed.

In the above photo, my camera had a 300mm f5.6 lens on it and was sitting 6 feet from the TP (Target Point). The DOF was calculated to be .3 inches (less than 1/2 inch). This gave me a very narrow margin for error, but because it was all calculated and manually set, I had pretty good success.

During the photo session I also set the camera to do some autofocus shots, setting the focus target on the anticipated TP. When you do this, be sure the bird has landed before suppressing the shutter release of the camera, otherwise the camera will try to focus on infinity. You also might change the focus area to center weight. This gives the sensors in the autofocus screen more area to look at.

Having some technical understanding helps, but it still takes a lot of trial and error. Again practice makes perfect. Don't be afraid of taking a bad shot. You learn more as you go.

6

Equipment

Camera

The most obvious starting place is the camera. It is recommended that you use a DSLR [Digital Single Lens Reflex] camera for several reasons. The first and most important reason is that you can change the lens. Using a larger zoom or telephoto lens will give you a distinct advantage in capturing the bird's image. Secondly, most newer DSLRs have some form of remote control so that you can take the picture while being away from the camera.

Lenses

Lens magnification is usually determined by factors of 50mm. In other words, a 50mm lens is 1X, 200mm lens is 4X, 300 mm lens is 6X and so on. For starting out, a standard 200mm zoom lens will work great. Remember a 200mm lens on a Dx format camera is equivalent to a 300mm lens because of the crop factor.

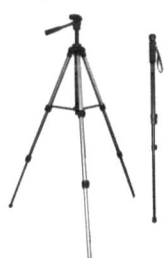

Stabilization

You will need a good tripod for camera support. It doesn't need to be a very expensive one, but it needs to be strong enough to hold your camera and lens. I also recommend getting a monopod.

Remote Shutter Release

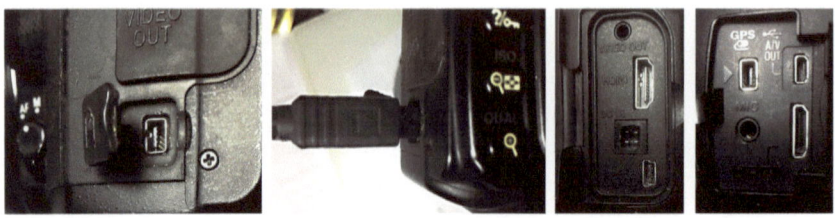

This depends on your camera and what kinds of remote shutter release features it has. Although most DSLRs have IR remote control, unless the IR sensor is on the back of the camera, it is going to be hard to do a setup. IR (infrared) sensors are line-of-sight, so when the sensor is on the front, it's harder not to disturb the target while snapping the shot. It is possible to position the camera so you actuate the IR sensor, but you will be very limited in how to set up the TP prop.

I like to use a shutter release cable plugged into the camera. A lot of the newer cameras have this feature. I use a 20-foot release cable that I bought on eBay. With this length I can sit inside and look out a window, snapping the photo when the bird 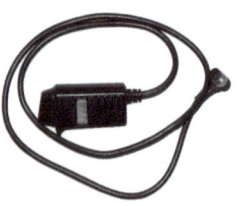 arrives at the TP. I use a shorter cable when I am sitting behind the camera using a monopod. It is more comfortable to use the cable than to hold up your hand the entire time you are waiting.

Flash

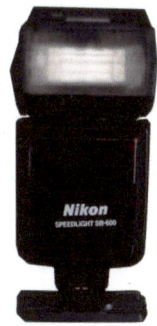

As mentioned earlier, I like to use fill flash on almost all of the bird photography I do. In most cases the pop-up flash on the camera is more than enough to provide fill flash on the subject. If you use larger lenses and plan to be more than 10 feet away from the bird, then I recommend buying a good exterior flash unit. Remember all of the flash will be set using manual control so you don't need a fancy TTL flash unit. Just make sure it has the ability to set its flash powers manually.

Tethering

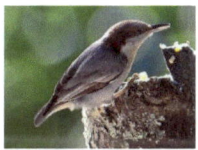 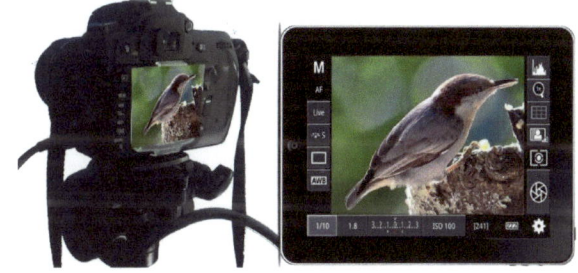

Tethering is when you hook your camera up to a device (Android, PC, Laptop), which allows you to control the camera with that device. With the release of newer cameras, many are now capable of doing this. There are several Android and Windows apps that will allow you to do this. Each camera manufacturer has its own way of doing it. From the remote, you can view the TP live, adjust camera settings, and take photos or video. In most cases the pictures or videos are transferred to the device for viewing and editing.

I will not go into detail on how to do this. There are lots of tutorials on YouTube if you are interested. I just wanted to let you know of the availability of this technology.

Teleconverter

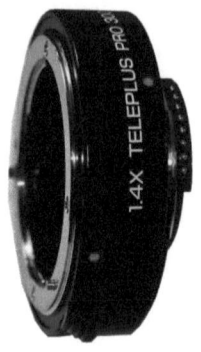 Teleconverters are small lenses which insert between the lens and the camera to increase the magnification of the lens. They are rated by their magnification power. When you use a teleconverter, it will change the f-stop rating of your lens because the lens in the teleconverter absorbs part of the light. A 1.4X teleconverter used on an f-4 300mm lens will change the effective settings to f5.6 420mm lens. When you use this on a DX formatted camera it will be equivalent to an f5.6 630mm lens.

7

Post Editing and Final Step

Once you have taken a series of photographs, you are going to want to transfer the photos to your computer or tablet for post processing. It is in post processing that you can really enhance and improve your photographs for a final spectacular look. I use Adobe Lightroom and Photoshop, as well as Nikon Capture NX2, and Perfect Effects 9. There are many photograph editing software products made for Windows and Apple applications.

The most common editing I do in post processing is cropping the photograph to give the best image composition, and adjusting the exposure (halftones, shadows, darks) to give the exposure effect I want. I also like to sharpen the images in post processing. Occasionally I will apply preset filter effects and borders on the photographs to bring out different looks.

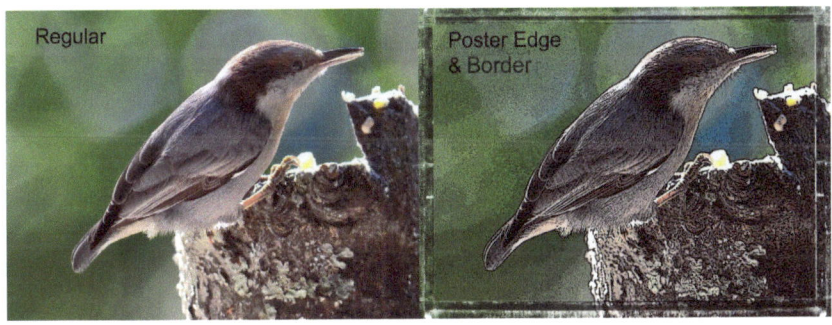

The Final Step

Now you have done it. The final step is to show off your work. Find your greatest photograph (and that will change with time) and share it on Social Media or have it printed (poster size) and framed. When your friends come to visit, they will be amazed.

Remember this process is an upward spiral. The more you do, the more you learn; the more you learn, the more you do. As you grow in your skills you will pay more attention to background, settings, and ways to capture the unusual. I hope this guide will get you started. It was not intended for a tell all, but to give you the basic tools to become a wonderful and satisfied Backyard Bird Photographer.

8

Some of My Favorite Setups

Using Remote

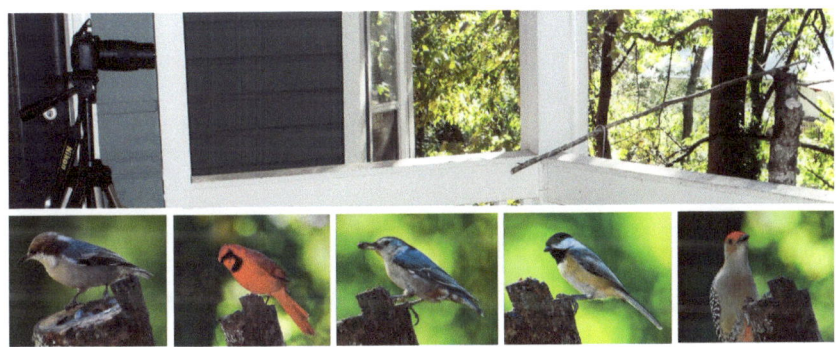

I have the highest percent of success when I use a remote shutter release because I can hide, making the birds more at ease. All the photographs above were taken in one session within one hour. I took down the hanging feeder while I was photographing in order to force the birds to go to the prop TP on which my camera was aimed. I prefocused to the center of the top using autofocus, then switched the focus control to manual. In the last four pictures I had rotated the trunk prop to hide the Sunflower seeds.

Camera	Nikon D80
Lens	Nikon 55-300mm f 5.6 (set at 200mm)
Stabilization	Tripod
Program Setting	Aperture
ISO	400 ISO
Aperture	f5-f5.4
Shutter Speed	1/60 sec
DOF	Calculated 1.2 to 1.4 inches
Metering	Pre-determined taking test shots
Focus	Pre-set using test target at TP, or Autofocus using center weight
Flash Setting	1/8
Shutter Control	Remote shutter release cable
Distance to TP	7 feet
Picture Setting	Large - Save in JPEG & RAW for post processing
Camouflage	Sometimes I will drape a camouflage T-shirt over camera (Not this time)

Using a 20-foot shutter release, I could sit inside the house and watch from the window, snapping the shutter when my guests arrived for their meal.

Sometimes I shoot both with preset focus and autofocus set on center weight aimed at the TP. When I use autofocus I make sure the bird is in the TP zone before I activate the shutter. The reason I like prefocus better is because you can take the photograph faster (don't have to wait for the camera to focus). Sometimes the birds don't stay long, so you need to be quick.

I have also had some success using a 55mm lens with the camera set about 18-24 inches away from the TP. If you try this, be aware of how the camera will focus on the bird once it is in the TP. If you use autofocus, be sure that you use center weight and not spot.

Behind the Camera

When possible I like to be behind the camera so I can look through the viewfinder and focus and position on the bird. To do this I need to be far enough away from the birds so as not to spook them. Some birds are skittish and won't come up if you are sitting there. In those cases, use a remote.

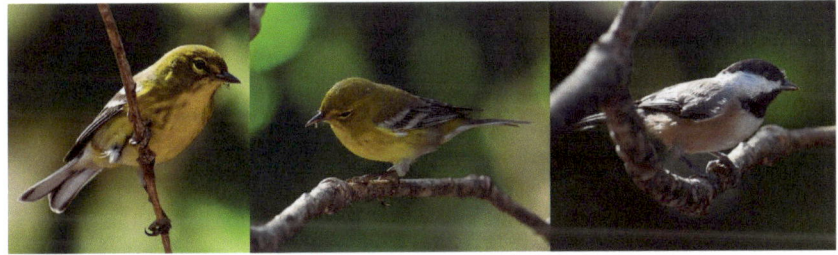

I photographed this Pine Warbler and Chickadee the same afternoon I photographed the birds shown above. You can see the small tree branch I have wire-tied to the back porch rail. These small props are great for behind the camera shots. As mentioned earlier, birds fly to these perches before flying over to the feeders. I was 9 feet away and behind the camera when the warbler flew in to get some seeds. With my camera on a tripod, I just aimed, focused, and snapped the photograph.

Here are the setups I used for these photographs.

Camera	Nikon D80
Lens	Nikon 55-300mm f 5.6 (set at 220mm f5.3)
Stabilization	Tripod
Program Setting	Shutter Preferred
ISO	400 ISO
Aperture	F5.3
DOF	Calculated 1.2 inches
Shutter Speed	1/60
Metering	Auto - Spot or Center Weight
Focus	Autofocus - Spot or Center Weight
Flash Setting	1/8
Shutter Control	Behind the camera - manual
Distance to TP	9 feet
Picture Setting	Large -Save in JPEG & RAW for post processing

9

Conclusion

I hope that through this guide you have learned some tips and techniques which will help to either start a new adventure or add to the one you are already enjoying in bird photography. With all the business and confusion that is around us, getting away for awhile to photograph these little visitors to a backyard feeder can be a great stress reliever. With a little setup you can become a renowned bird photographer and share this joy with others.

If you have found this guide useful, please recommend it to others. My hope is that you will continue in this hobby and enjoy it as much as I do.

In this quest there will be many throwaways, but also many keepers. As you do more of it you will develop your own methodology. Keep notes on things you have learned and insert them into your technique.

Thank you, and may God bless.

Be sure to join our Facebook Group:

Backyard Bird Photography.

https://www.facebook.com/groups/200077663749673/

There you may ask questions and share your techniques. You also may share your photos – and see those of others. Hope to see you there.

About the Author

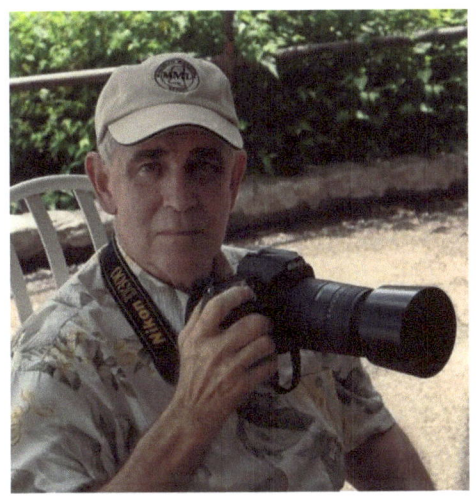 Mickey Estes is an ordained minister who has led a more-than-busy life for decades. As such, he has learned to squeeze out some relaxation by enjoying nature – many times with a camera in hand. One of his specialties has been drawing birds to his backyard, and photographing them. Over the years, Mickey has learned many tricks which have produced first class photos.

Thousands of his bird shots have been downloaded from photo websites, such as Pixabay. Many have been used in blogs, websites, and publications. Other photos have received recognition from the Shiloh Eagle Watchers and Cornell Lab of Ornithology. Most of his photos have just been enjoyed by family and friends.

This book is a culmination of ideas and techniques Mickey has used for his award-winning photos. With a little training and practice, you too can enjoy this relaxing and profitable hobby.

www.ingramcontent.com/pod-product-compliance
Lightning Source LLC
Chambersburg PA
CBHW040846180526
45159CB00001B/338